THE BATTLE OF LITTLE BIGHORN

LEGENDARY BATTLE OF THE GREAT SIOUX WAR

by Katy Duffield

D0123648

FOCUS READERS

WWW.NORTHSTAREDITIONS.COM

Produced for North Star Editions by Red Line Editorial.

Photographs ©: National Geographic Creative/Alamy, cover, 1; Jun Kawaguchi/Shutterstock Images, 5; Chuck Haney/Danita Delimont Photography/Newscom, 6–7; Everett Historical/ Shutterstock Images, 9; Don Mammoser/Shutterstock Images, 10; North Wind Picture Archive, 12–13; Alexander Gardner/akg-images/Newscom, 15; akg-images/Newscom, 18–19, 24–25; Smith Collection/Gado/Archive Photos/Getty Images, 21; Stapleton Historical Collection Heritage Images/Newscom, 23; Red Line Editorial 27, 29

Content Consultant: Leila Monaghan, PhD, Visiting Assistant Professor of Anthropology at Southern Illinois University

ISBN
978-1-63517-020-7 (hardcover)
978-1-63517-076-4 (paperback)
978-1-63517-180-8 (ebook pdf)
978-1-63517-130-3 (hosted ebook)

Library of Congress Control Number: 2016949832

Printed in the United States of America
Mankato, MN
November, 2016

ABOUT THE AUTHOR

Katy Duffield has a bachelor's degree in English from the University of Illinois–Springfield. She is the author of more than 20 books for children and has written both fiction and nonfiction for many children's magazines.

TABLE OF CONTENTS

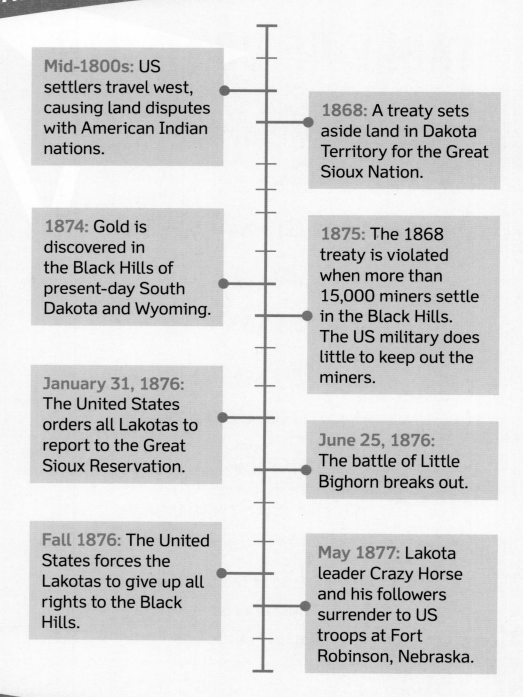

Mid-1800s: US settlers travel west, causing land disputes with American Indian nations.

1868: A treaty sets aside land in Dakota Territory for the Great Sioux Nation.

1874: Gold is discovered in the Black Hills of present-day South Dakota and Wyoming.

1875: The 1868 treaty is violated when more than 15,000 miners settle in the Black Hills. The US military does little to keep out the miners.

January 31, 1876: The United States orders all Lakotas to report to the Great Sioux Reservation.

June 25, 1876: The battle of Little Bighorn breaks out.

Fall 1876: The United States forces the Lakotas to give up all rights to the Black Hills.

May 1877: Lakota leader Crazy Horse and his followers surrender to US troops at Fort Robinson, Nebraska.

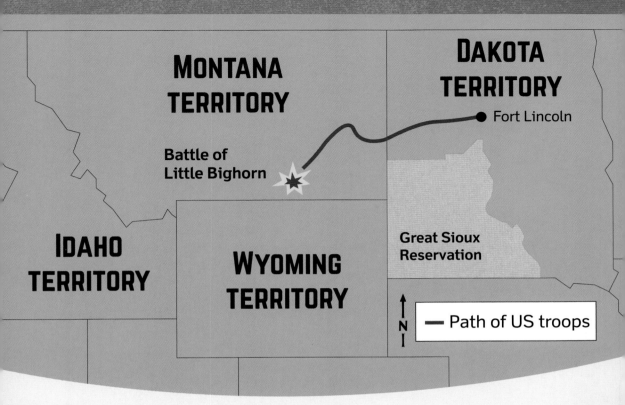

BATTLE OF LITTLE BIGHORN

	US Soldiers	Lakota, Cheyenne, and Arapaho Warriors
Leaders	George Armstrong Custer, Frederick Benteen, and Marcus Reno	Sitting Bull, Crazy Horse, and Gall
Total Strength	647	900–2,000
Killed	268	40–60
Wounded	55	160

CHAPTER 1

ATTACK AT GREASY GRASS

On June 25, 1876, Moving Robe Woman was a few miles from her camp in Montana Territory. She and other Lakota women were digging for turnips when they noticed a cloud of dust rising beyond a nearby ridge. Suddenly, a Lakota **warrior** raced toward them on horseback.

Lakotas and Cheyennes were holding a ceremony near the Little Bighorn River in June 1876.

The warrior shouted that US soldiers were coming to attack. He told the women to take the children and run in the opposite direction. Moving Robe saw soldiers on horseback on a bluff across the Little Bighorn River, which the Lakotas called the Greasy Grass. Instead of running for the hills, Moving Robe ran back to camp. As word of the attack spread, commotion filled the camp. Moving Robe's father ran to gather the horses. Pistol and rifle fire rang out as US soldiers shot into the camp.

Inside her family's tent, Moving Robe's mother shared horrible news. The attacking soldiers had killed One Hawk,

US soldiers attack the Lakota camp.

Moving Robe's brother. Moving Robe was heartbroken. She stopped long enough to sing a death song for her brother. But she wanted to do more than sing for her brother. She also wanted to help protect the Lakotas' land.

A memorial now sits at the site of the battle.

Moving Robe braided her hair and painted her face red, representing strength and energy. She climbed onto her black pony and joined her father and hundreds of other Lakota warriors. They were armed with rifles, bows and arrows, and war clubs. When the command was given, the warriors thundered toward the invading soldiers from all directions. War cries rang out. Gunshots and arrows filled the air. The Lakota charge forced the US soldiers to **retreat**. Moving Robe and the Lakota warriors chased the soldiers back across the river to the other side of a bluff. Moving Robe and the warriors were proud of their victory. They stopped to sing a victory song.

But they knew the battle was far from over. Another group of US soldiers was attacking the other side of the village. Moving Robe, her father, and the other warriors raced into the dust and toward the gunfire.

CHAPTER 2

LAND CLASH

In the mid-1800s, the United States was expanding. People from the East wanted to explore the West. They hoped to find better lives there. But there was a problem with this plan. As settlers moved west, they took land that did not belong to them.

US settlers moved onto lands that were already in use.

The Lakotas and other northern plains tribes had lived for generations in the area known to US settlers as Dakota Territory. But this did not stop settlers from living on the land. They invaded the Lakotas' homes and hunting grounds. They **trespassed** on the Black Hills, a place the Lakotas view as sacred. The settlers' **disregard** for the Lakota way of life caused serious **clashes**.

US officials wanted to stop the fighting. They also wanted to control the Lakotas. So, in 1868, US officials wrote a **treaty**. The treaty set aside an area of land in Dakota Territory for the Lakotas and other American Indians to live on. The area was

Sioux, Arapaho, and Cheyenne leaders, among others, met with US leaders in Fort Laramie, Wyoming, in 1868.

called the Great Sioux **Reservation**. The treaty also stated that no outsiders could trespass or settle there. Many Lakotas moved to the reservation. Others did not.

Sitting Bull, an important Lakota leader, refused to live on the reservation.

He thought it was wrong to be forced onto a piece of land. He did not think the US government had the authority to tell the Lakotas where they could live and hunt.

In 1874, another problem arose in the US government's plan. US soldiers, trespassing on Lakota land, found gold

SITTING BULL

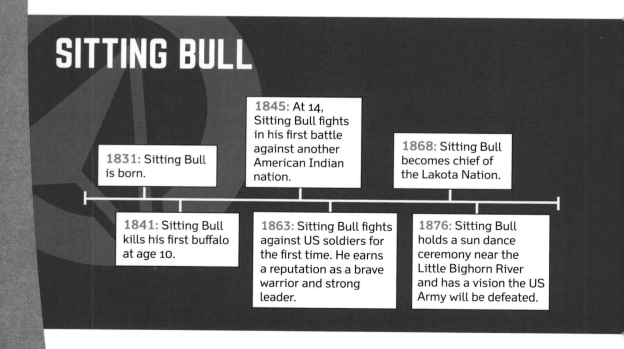

1831: Sitting Bull is born.

1841: Sitting Bull kills his first buffalo at age 10.

1845: At 14, Sitting Bull fights in his first battle against another American Indian nation.

1863: Sitting Bull fights against US soldiers for the first time. He earns a reputation as a brave warrior and strong leader.

1868: Sitting Bull becomes chief of the Lakota Nation.

1876: Sitting Bull holds a sun dance ceremony near the Little Bighorn River and has a vision the US Army will be defeated.

in the Black Hills of Dakota Territory. Thousands of US miners flocked to the area. They hoped to become rich by finding and selling gold. The miners scarred and trampled the Lakotas' sacred land. The treaty between the Lakotas and the US government made the miners' actions illegal. But the US government did little to keep the trespassers out of the Black Hills.

After the gold discovery, US president Ulysses S. Grant wanted to buy back the Black Hills. But Sitting Bull and other Lakotas refused. Sitting Bull insisted his sacred homeland was not for sale.

CHAPTER 3

THE BATTLE BEGINS

US officials were not happy when Sitting Bull refused to sell the Black Hills. So they issued new orders. All Lakotas and their Northern Cheyenne allies were required to report to the reservation by January 31, 1876. Then in February, US soldiers moved into the area to enforce the US demands.

Sitting Bull's reputation as a leader drew people from other tribes to his camp.

On March 17, a US Army unit led by Colonel Joseph J. Reynolds attacked a Northern Cheyenne village located outside the reservation. The village was destroyed. The Northern Cheyenne men, women, and children found shelter at Sitting Bull's camp off of the reservation. Lakotas, Northern Cheyennes, and Arapahos also traveled to the camp for a religious ceremony called a sun dance.

Meanwhile, three large groups of US soldiers moved through the region. On June 17, warriors from Sitting Bull's camp attacked a group of US soldiers led by Brigadier General George Crook. Crazy Horse, a well-known Lakota warrior, led

American Indian families in Sitting Bull's camp in 1875

the attack, which forced Crook's soldiers to withdraw. After the battle, Sitting Bull moved his camp. He settled northwest near the Little Bighorn River.

On June 25, a US Army unit led by Lieutenant Colonel George Armstrong Custer located Sitting Bull's camp.

Instead of waiting for more US troops to arrive, Custer decided to attack. Custer divided his 650 soldiers into three battle groups. Each group would attack from a different direction. Sitting Bull was ready for the attack. Approximately 1,500 to 2,000 Lakota, Northern Cheyenne, and Arapaho warriors were prepared to fight. Crazy Horse and Gall, another Lakota war leader, helped organize the warriors.

Custer first ordered Major Marcus Reno and his group of 131 men to attack Sitting Bull's camp. Reno's soldiers put up a fight. But they were quickly met by hundreds of warriors, whose rapid-fire rifles and arrows overwhelmed

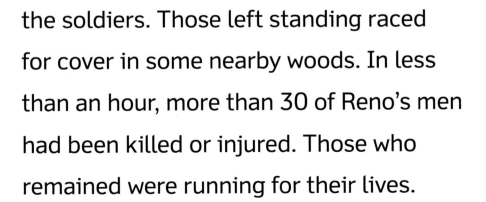

A pictograph shows Marcus Reno's troops retreating across the Little Bighorn River.

the soldiers. Those left standing raced for cover in some nearby woods. In less than an hour, more than 30 of Reno's men had been killed or injured. Those who remained were running for their lives.

CHAPTER 4

FIGHTING TO SURVIVE

As Reno and his men fought, Custer's group continued toward the Lakota camp from another direction. Custer and his soldiers climbed a hill that sat above the Little Bighorn River. The hill provided a view of the Lakota village below. The village was much bigger than Custer had expected.

Custer ignored an order to wait for additional troops before attacking Sitting Bull's camp.

Custer sent a message to Captain Frederick Benteen, the leader of the third attack party. Custer said he needed more soldiers to attack a village so large. Benteen's group never arrived. Custer and his men tried to flee. But hundreds of Lakota fighters charged at them from behind. In front, Crazy Horse stood with 1,000 other warriors, ready for battle.

Battle cries and gunshots filled the air. Custer and his men returned fire, but they were heavily outnumbered. Warriors galloped toward Custer's group. They attacked with arrows, hatchets, clubs, and bullets. In less than 30 minutes, Custer and all 210 men in his group were dead.

The battle of Little Bighorn was a big win for the northern plains tribes. More than 250 US soldiers were killed. The battle was also costly for the Lakotas, Northern Cheyennes, and Arapahos. They lost between 40 and 60 warriors. But they had defended their land.

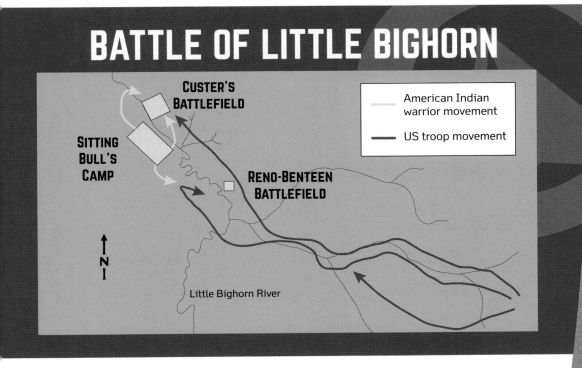

BATTLE OF LITTLE BIGHORN

CUSTER'S
BATTLEFIELD

SITTING
BULL'S
CAMP

RENO-BENTEEN
BATTLEFIELD

American Indian
warrior movement

US troop movement

N

Little Bighorn River

News of Custer's defeat made its way east. US citizens were shocked and outraged by what they believed to be a **massacre**. They did not understand that the warriors at Sitting Bull's camp had been defending their homeland.

In August 1876, a new law was passed. The United States forced the Lakotas to give up all claims to the Black Hills. The Lakotas were also made to surrender the rights to their hunting grounds outside the reservation.

Though the Lakotas won on the battlefield of Little Bighorn, their fight was far from over. During the next several years, the United States forced the

Lakotas back onto the reservation and took away their guns and horses. Today, Lakotas are still struggling to regain the Black Hills.

LOST LAND

This map shows the difference in size between the Great Sioux Reservation of 1868 and the boundaries of reservations in the region today.

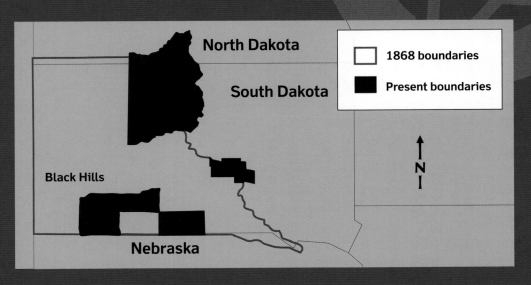

North Dakota

South Dakota

Black Hills

Nebraska

☐ 1868 boundaries

■ Present boundaries

N ↑

FOCUS ON
THE BATTLE OF LITTLE BIGHORN

Write your answers on a separate piece of paper.

1. Summarize Chapter 2 of this book.

2. Why do you think the US government did not stop people from trespassing on the Black Hills?

3. What is another name for the Little Bighorn River?

    A. the Dakota

    B. the Missouri

    C. the Greasy Grass

4. Which of these may have been a reason US citizens thought of the battle of Little Bighorn as a massacre?

    A. They heard only the US military's version of the battle.

    B. They heard only the Lakotas' version of the battle.

    C. They sympathized with the American Indians who were being forced to move.

Answer key on page 32.

GLOSSARY

clashes
Short fights between groups of people.

disregard
The act of treating something as unimportant.

massacre
The violent killing of many people.

reservation
An area of land set aside for American Indian people.

retreat
When soldiers move away from battle.

treaty
An official agreement between groups.

trespassed
To have gone onto someone's land without permission.

warrior
A person who fights in battles.

TO LEARN MORE

BOOKS

Higgins, Nadia. *Last Stand: Causes and Effects of the Battle of the Little Bighorn.* North Mankato, MN: Capstone, 2015.

Roxburgh, Ellis. *Sitting Bull vs. George Armstrong Custer.* New York: Gareth Stevens, 2016.

Spinner, Stephanie. *Who Was Sitting Bull?* New York: Grosset & Dunlap, 2014.

NOTE TO EDUCATORS

Visit **www.focusreaders.com** to find lesson plans, activities, links, and other resources related to this title.

INDEX

Answer Key: 1. Answers will vary; **2.** Answers will vary; **3.** C; **4.** A